PAPA
Didn't Understand

JESUS WAS YOUR AGE

DORIS C. SHOLLY

Library of Congress Control Number: 2022902012

PAPERBACK: 978-1-957575-29-2
EBOOK: 978-1-957575-30-8

Ordering Information:

For orders and inquiries, please contact:
1-888-404-1388
www.goldtouchpress.com
book.orders@goldtouchpress.com

Printed in the United States of America

This book Belongs
To ___________________________

Who lives at

____

____

I am ________ Years old

From ___________________________

Given to me on this day

____

Dedication

I want to dedicate these books to all the children everywhere. I want you to remember Jesus was your age, and He was tempted like you are – "...yet without sin." Hebrews 4:15b. He is able to help you with your temptations so you don't have to sin. If you do sin, ask Jesus to forgive you of your sins. I John 1:9.

I want to thank everyone who encouraged me in the writing and helping with the correcting of the books.

The people from Author House were really an encouragement to me. They kept me pushing.

I hope these books are a help to children, Sunday School Teachers, and parents everywhere.

Doris Sholly

"It is time for supper, Papa," little 2 year old Joses announced as Jesus, James, and Joses came into the carpenter's shop.

"Thank you for coming to tell me. It is such a big help so Mother doesn't have to leave Baby Hannah to come to tell me," Papa said.

"We're having vegetables from the garden," James said. "I helped pull the carrots."

"I am sure you did a good job." Papa exclaimed.

"That sounds good, and I have something for my three big helpers. Jesus here is a donkey for You; James, here is a dog for you, and Joses, I made you a little lamb,"

"Now let's go see how good Mother fixed those carrots." Papa said as he picked up four year old James and little Joses.

"Thank you for the donkey." Jesus said. Then ran to to open the door for Papa and the boys.

"Thank you for holding the door open that is a big help when I have my arms full of boys," "Mmmm, it smells good in here," Papa said as he put the boys down.

"Mmmm, I smell carrots," James said.

"Mmmm, I smell Mama," Joses said.

"See what Papa gave me! I got a dog, Jesus got a donkey, and Joses got a lamb," James said and was all out of breath.

"James, I wanted to tell Mother 'out my lamb," Joses said with a pout.

"Come, we must wash our hands before we eat," Papa said.

Soon everyone was at the table. Papa said the blessing before they started to eat.

"I like to look at the little blocks of wood after I have made something and think about what I could make out of them," Papa said.

"Sometimes I will give my little boys some of them, but not every time." "I like that idea," Mother said. "Is that how I got my cup rack?"

Papa grinned and said, "Yes, that board looked like a good board for you to hang up your cups."

"Thank you for telling me that. Now I will appreciate it that much more," Mother said.

After supper, the boys had fun playing with their new carved animals, and the next morning they went out to the dirt pile with their animals. After they played awhile, James said, "Let's go see Papa in the shop."

Jesus opened the door and then said, "Papa is not here; we must go back and play."

"Papa said we are his big helpers, so maybe we can help him," James said. "See here is a nice board and here is a hammer," he said as he stepped to the board on the stump.

"No, put it back," Jesus said.

"Here is my little hammer, Papa lets me use and some nails." Joses said. "Bang, bang," went James hammer.

"No, no," Jesus said. "Put them back Papa is not here." Then he took the board from James and put it on the beach.

"Bang, bang, bang," went Joses' hammer making holes in the board.

"I said, 'No, we must wait for Papa,'" Jesus said. He took the hammer and nails from Joses and turned around.

Just then Papa walked in the door and said cheerily, "What are my helpers doing?"

"Oh! No! you have spoiled the chair seat. I worked so hard to finish; now it is ruined." He scolded Jesus, James and Joses. "Now you go and don't come in here unless Mother tells you to come, and if I am not here, don't come in. You hear me all of you! Jesus, you know better than to do this!" Papa was upset. "Now all of you go!"

Two crying boys went to the house – to Mother.

Jesus went to the goat shed where He talked with His Father, "Father help Me understand even when Papa doesn't understand Me." As He talked with His Father, a peace came into His heart, "I love Thee, Father," Jesus said before He went to the house.

$\mathbf{W}$hen Jesus was on the step, he heard Papa saying, "You said Jesus is not here? Where is He pouting this time?" (Jesus did not pout, but Papa thought He was pouting.)

"I was in the goat shed talking to My Father," Jesus said.

"You were in the goat shed?" Papa said as he took Him by the arm. "I don't want you pouting anymore."

"Papa, He has not been pouting. Look at the radiance on His face," Mother said.

"What did You say You were doing in the goat shed?"

"I was talking to My Father," Jesus answered.

"How could You talk to 'Your Father' in the goat shed when Papa was in the shop?" James asked. "Papa, why did you scold Jesus in the shop? He didn't do anything bad. He just took the hammer and nails from Joses to go put them away."

"I am sorry, Jesus," Papa said. "I should have asked what was happening. I am sorry I lost my temper. Please forgive me.

"James, I am your father, but I am not Jesus' father. I am only His stepfather. God, Jehovah is His Father. Thank You Jesus for reminding me."

"Papa, God the Father has a better way for you to live so you don't have to lose your temper," Jesus said.

"Jesus, pray for us," Joseph said and they all knelt to pray.

Do you think Jesus might have prayed something like this: "Father, Thou art so great, and Thou art so able to help us with all of our problems. Help Papa and Mother to understand Thy Ways more perfectly. Help them to love Thee more. Help James and Joses to love Thee. Help us all to do Thy Will, Amen."

This is a Series of Books About Jesus as a Boy

Entitled: JESUS WAS YOUR AGE

Book 1 – BECAUSE HE LOVED US!

Jesus loved us so much that He came to earth to live as we live. This book is when Jesus was a Baby until they came back from Egypt

Book 2 –
PAPA DIDN'T UNDERSTAND

Jesus was 9 years old. What were Jesus half brothers doing that it looked like Jesus was doing it too?

Book 3 –
JESUS WAS A HELPER

Jesus was about 11 playing with the other children, but was ready to help where He could. Sometimes He saw things that needed to be done, and sometimes He came up with some different ideas. Find out how!

Book 4 –
WHAT WOULD JESUS DO?

Jesus was a young teenager, and when He met up with problems, what do you suppose He did?

Book 5 –
JESUS TOOK OVER

Jesus was an older teenager and into His twenties. Joseph was sick and Jesus had to take over in the carpenter's shop. He had to teach James, Joses, & Jude, His half brothers. The four of them had to do all the work.

Written and illustrated by
Mrs. Doris C. Sholly
Mapril Press
214 N. 12th Street Fredonia,
KS 66736